CHILDREN NEED
WATER

Wendy Davies

THE WORLD'S CHILDREN

Children Need Education
Children Need Families
Children Need Food
Children Need A Future
Children Need Health Care
Children Need Homes
Children Need Recreation
Children Need Water

Series Editor: Stephen White-Thomson
Book Editor: Rosemary Ashley
Consultant: Save the Children

All words that appear in bold in the text are explained in the glossary on page 44.

First published in 1988 by
Wayland (Publishers) Limited
61 Western Road, Hove
East Sussex BN3 1JD, England

British Library Cataloguing in Publication Data
Davies, Wendy
    Children need water. – (The World's
    children)
    1. Water – Juvenile literature
    I. Title   II. Series
    553.7   GB662.3

    ISBN 1–85210–270–5

Phototypeset by Kalligraphics Ltd, Redhill, Surrey
Printed in Italy by G. Canale & C.S.p.A, Turin
Bound in Belgium by Casterman SA, Tournai

Front cover: Peruvian schoolchildren now have fresh, clean water piped to their school.

Back cover: Even young members of families in South-east Asia help with collecting water from the village well.

Title page: Water brings enjoyment to many people besides being essential for survival: these children are having fun in a swimming pool in England.

Contents page: A young Indian girl carries a heavy bowl of water on her head.

CONTENTS

THE RIGHTS OF THE CHILD

Eglantine Jebb, the founder of The Save the Children Fund, drafted the Rights of the Child in 1923. It was revised in 1948 by the present Declaration of the Rights of the Child, commonly known as the Declaration of Geneva. These principles form the basis of our work and the Charter of The Save the Children Fund.

1 The Child must be protected beyond and above all considerations of race, nationality or creed.

2 The Child must be cared for with due respect for the family as an entity.

3 The Child must be given the means requisite for its normal development, materially, morally and spiritually.

4 The Child that is hungry must be fed, the child that is sick must be nursed, the child that is mentally or physically handicapped must be helped, the maladjusted child must be re-educated, the orphan and the waif must be sheltered and succoured.

5 The Child must be the first to receive relief in time of distress.

6 The Child must enjoy the full benefits provided by social welfare and social security schemes, must receive a training which will enable it, at the right time, to earn a livelihood, and must be protected against every form of exploitation.

7 The Child must be brought up in the consciousness that its talents must be devoted to the service of its fellow men.

BUCKINGHAM PALACE

All children, regardless of race, nationality or creed, have basic rights. These rights were outlined by Eglantine Jebb, the founder of Save the Children, in 1923 and they have now become an integral part of the United Nations charter. You can read them on the opposite page.

I welcome this thought-provoking series and applaud the way it confronts the issues facing today's children throughout the world. In the end we are all part of the same human race, and not so different from one another. Where differences do exist, they enrich us.

As Britain's largest international children's charity, Save the Children works where there is real need, both in the UK and in over 50 countries around the world. The idea behind all our projects is to encourage people to help themselves. But SCF also accepts its responsibility to talk about the issues of world-wide child poverty - particularly to the young - which makes this work so necessary. This series is designed to do just that.

I am sure that this colourful series will be an invaluable resource for any school whose aim is to make their pupils think beyond the confines of their playground and their community. We are one world after all. Let's try and be one.

Anne

THE WORLD'S WATER

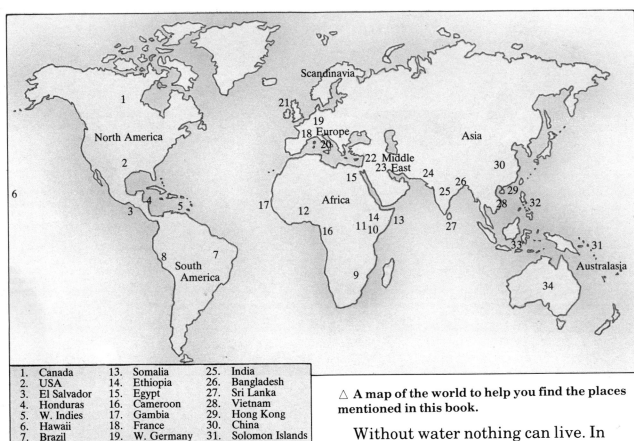

1.	Canada	13.	Somalia	25.	India
2.	USA	14.	Ethiopia	26.	Bangladesh
3.	El Salvador	15.	Egypt	27.	Sri Lanka
4.	Honduras	16.	Cameroon	28.	Vietnam
5.	W. Indies	17.	Gambia	29.	Hong Kong
6.	Hawaii	18.	France	30.	China
7.	Brazil	19.	W. Germany	31.	Solomon Islands
8.	Peru	20.	Italy	32.	Philippines
9.	Zimbabwe	21.	Britain	33.	Indonesia
10.	Kenya	22.	Syria	34.	Australia
11.	Uganda	23.	Iraq		
12.	Burkina Faso	24.	Pakistan		

△ **A map of the world to help you find the places mentioned in this book.**

Water is the most common substance on Earth. It covers about 70 per cent of our planet's surface, and most of it – about 97 per cent – is in the oceans. The rest is in rivers, streams, lakes, waterfalls, pools, ponds and puddles. Water falls as rain or – in solid form – as snow, sleet or hail. It is frozen in the ice-caps and glaciers of the Arctic and Antarctic, and is found beneath the Earth's surface, in underground lakes and rivers, or in layers of **porous** rock.

Without water nothing can live. In fact, life on Earth is believed by most scientists to have begun in the oceans. Living things actually consist mainly of water – our bodies, for example are two-thirds water – and depend on it to survive. Water is so important because it dissolves essential **nutrients** and carries them to all the tiny cells that make up plants, animals and human beings.

The food we eat contains large quantities of water, too. Bananas may not seem a particularly juicy fruit but they are 75 per cent water; cabbages are 92 per cent water; even something as dry as oats contains 5 per cent water.

Water shapes the world we live in. The sea pounds against the coasts, sweeping land away and carving out steep cliffs. Rivers erode the soil and wash down silt from the higher ground. Millions of years ago, during the ice ages, glaciers moved over vast areas of the Earth, creating mountains and valleys and transforming the shape of the land.

The survival and development of entire peoples is affected by water. Societies have flourished in the valleys of great rivers – the Nile Valley in Egypt, for example, or the Indus Valley in Pakistan – and have crumbled when water supplies failed or were poorly managed.

△ **Water crashes over the Niagara Falls, in Canada, and flows to the sea.**

Nearly three-quarters of the Earth's surface is covered by water. ▽

BABIES AND WATER

Even before a human being takes its first breath of life, it is familiar with water as a substance. For nine months the developing **foetus** floats in a bag of watery liquid, known as amniotic fluid. The fluid protects the foetus from any knocks and bumps during the later stages of pregnancy. When a baby is ready to be born, the cushion of amniotic fluid bursts, and he or she is pushed out into the world. One of the baby's first experiences of life is being washed with water by the birth attendant, midwife, doctor or nurse.

▽ **The foetus floats in its watery bag of amniotic fluid.**

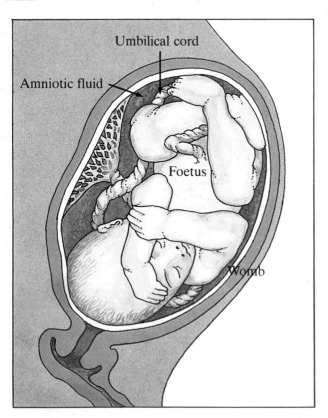

Umbilical cord

Amniotic fluid

Foetus

Womb

For the first few months of its life a baby will feed only on milk and water. Unlike cow's milk, the mother's milk is not too rich for the baby's sensitive digestive system to cope with. It is exactly what the baby needs as it contains less **protein**, more sugar and more water than cow's milk. If breast-feeding is impossible, babies are bottle-fed with cow's milk which has been diluted with water.

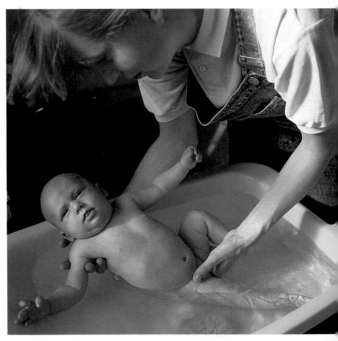

Most babies really enjoy bath time! They are quite fearless of water even when it is poured over their heads. Very small babies can learn to swim long before they can walk, or even crawl. This may seem remarkable, but when you think of the foetus 'swimming' in the womb, it is not so surprising.

△ (above left) Most small babies enjoy their bath and the pleasant sensation of being immersed in water.

△ A young Ethiopian mother washes her baby's head. Contact with water is one of the first experiences that a new-born baby undergoes.

THE BODY NEEDS WATER

△ We need to drink 1.5 litres of water every day to stay healthy. Without water we would survive for only a few days.

The body needs 1.5 litres of water a day. We can survive up to a few weeks without food but only a matter of days without water. So why is water so important to our bodies?

The millions of tiny cells which make up the human body contain a large amount of water. The water in the bloodstream dissolves nutrients needed by all the body's cells and tissues and carries them to each part of the body. Food is turned into energy by a chemical process that can only take place in a watery solution.

Your eyes need water, too. The eyeball is moistened and protected by a thin layer of salty water which is released by the **lachrymal gland**. If a speck of dust gets in your eye, the amount of water (tears) increases and washes it away. So crying can be a way of cleansing your eyes, as well as an important way of releasing your feelings.

Water is also essential to the body because it carries away waste. All the water in the body is filtered by the kidneys, which cleanse impurities from the blood. Useful substances are retained in the blood, and waste is carried away as urine, which passes out of the bladder. The kidneys make sure you keep the right amount of water in your body. If there is too little water, your body becomes dehydrated – severe dehydration causes death. Loss of water in the body is the main danger from diarrhoea, a disease that kills 5 million babies and children in the developing world every year.

▽ Tears are salty water which protects the eyes and keeps them moist.

You lose water when you sweat. Moisture is released by the sweat glands on to the surface of the skin. There it evaporates, taking the heat from your body and cooling you down.

A young Indian girl washes her face at the tap outside her home. A good clean water supply helps to keep the body healthy. ▷

▽ People living in the Ogaden desert of Ethiopia have barely enough water to survive. If their supply dries up they may die.

WATER AT HOME

Think of the number of different ways in which you use water in your home. You wash your hands and face using water in a basin or from the running tap. You take showers or baths. You use water when you clean your teeth. Every time you flush the lavatory the cistern releases 10 litres of water to carry away the waste and clean out the bowl.

During the day you probably have several drinks, all of which are largely water. Water is also used in lots of ways for cooking. It is used for cleaning the house, for washing and rinsing clothes and doing the washing-up. Cars have to be cleaned regularly too. House-plants need to be watered and gardens require watering in dry weather.

△ Huge amounts of water are used in labour-saving devices like dishwashers.

△ One very usual way in which we all use water in our homes is for cleaning our teeth.

In developed countries more and more domestic gadgets are being produced that use large quantities of water. There are washing-machines, dishwashers, waste disposal units and garden sprinklers. Can you think of any more gadgets?

It takes about 110–150 litres of water to fill a bath, about 40 litres to take a 2-minute shower and up to 38 litres to wash dishes in a sink. An automatic washing-machine uses as much as 110 litres for one wash. People in developed countries use an average of 150 litres per person, per day. In the USA, where there are more kitchen taps and flush lavatories than in any other country, the average daily consumption is 260 litres per person.

In developing countries people have to manage with far less water. The average daily consumption is 12 litres per person, although it is officially estimated that each person needs 30–50 litres to stay clean and healthy. Only a small minority of people have water piped to their homes, and even then the supply may not

△ These Indian villagers cannot use water in the wasteful way it is sometimes used in developed countries.

be continuous. Many people have to take water from rivers which are polluted and are therefore serious health hazards. Wells, too, are often unreliable and contaminated.

13

WHERE DOES IT COME FROM?

All the water that we use in our daily lives has been used many, many times before, in a natural cycle as old as the Earth itself. How is this so?

Water goes round and round, falling as rain, flowing in rivers to the sea and rising into the atmosphere to form rain clouds again. This is called the water cycle.

If you put a bowl of water outside – keeping thirsty animals away in case they drink it – you will see that the water level gradually drops. The water does not actually vanish but the warmth from the sun's rays heats it and turns it into vapour in the air. This process, called evaporation, is what happens to water all over the surface of the Earth, in the seas, rivers and lakes.

When the water vapour rises above the Earth it meets cooler air higher up. It cools down and forms droplets of water which collect around particles of dust to produce clouds. As the clouds are blown over the land they cool still more and the larger drops of water fall as rain, or as hail, sleet or snow when it is very cold. The rain soaks into the ground, and comes to the surface again in springs and streams. Rivers and streams run into the sea, where the cycle begins again.

Rain does not fall in the same quantity everywhere. North-east India has 1,000 cm every year, but in northern Chile it often does not rain at all for several years.

▽ **Water falls as rain, flows into rivers and oceans, and rises again into the atmosphere to form clouds. This process is known as the water cycle.**

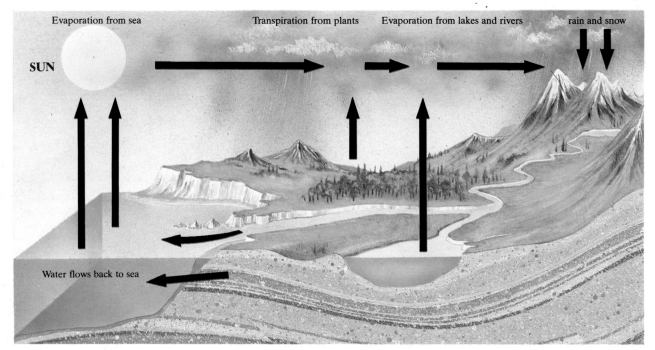

Evaporation from sea   Transpiration from plants   Evaporation from lakes and rivers   rain and snow

SUN

Water flows back to sea

△ Heavy rain clouds over Bangladesh during the monsoon season.

Sudden downpours in very dry areas can cause floods and landslides, which kill people and destroy their homes. A drought can sometimes occur in areas that normally have sufficient rain, and this may cause widespread famine.

Parts of the world have too much water – villages in the delta of the Brahmaputra River in Bangladesh are regularly flooded during the monsoon. ▷

Most of the usable fresh water in the world is underground. Even in very dry lands, when rivers and lakes disappear during the dry season, there is nearly always water to be found below the surface of the Earth. This is called the **water table**. Throughout history, people have invented new methods of drawing the water to the surface.

▽ Villagers in Somalia collecting water from an underground stream.

▽ Water from deep underground is drawn from this well in Pakistan.

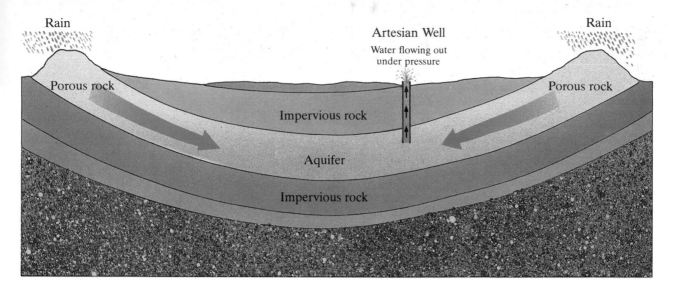

The Aborigines of Australia pierce a hole deep into the ground, and then fill it with dried grass. They force a hollow reed into the hole and use it like a drinking straw to suck up the water, which is filtered as it passes through the grass.

All over the developing world, people rely on wells. If the water table is near the surface, water can be hauled up by hand, but if it lies deeper down it has to be raised by means of a pump. By drilling to a deeper level it is often possible to find water sources close to villages.

Once, at Boroma refugee camp in Somalia, there was an acute shortage of water. The refugees dug into the dried-up river bed to find water, but the supply was very limited. Workers from Save the Children helped the refugees dig deeper wells so they could get more water. A local engineering firm, backed by the Intermediate Technology Development Group, recently installed a wind-pump near Lake Turkana in Kenya, to draw water from 200 metres below the ground. For the first time in their lives the nomadic people of the area had a plentiful supply of fresh water. On the first night 3,000 people queued up to collect some water.

△ An artesian basin, like the one under London.

A very large amount of water can be found underground in what is known as an **artesian basin**. In the hills at the edge of a basin, water enters a layer of porous rock between two **impermeable** layers. The porous layer in the basin becomes saturated and when a well is sunk into it, the water rushes upwards to ground level. London is built in an artesian basin.

▽ The wind pump near Lake Turkana in Kenya provides villagers with plenty of fresh water from deep underground.

DAILY SEARCH FOR WATER

There is an English nursery rhyme which begins, 'Jack and Jill went up the hill / To fetch a pail of water' – but nowadays there are very few places left in the developed world where children need go outside their own homes to fetch water.

▽ In Villa El Salvador, a poor area of Lima, Peru, water is delivered by lorry to a communal tank.

However, the vast majority of rural people in Africa, Asia and Latin America do not have running water in their homes. Along with the rest of their heavy work burden – including caring for children, cooking, fetching firewood, working in the fields – women are traditionally responsible for collecting water. Children often help their mothers with this task, or stay at home to look after their younger brothers and sisters while their mothers work.

The source of water is often a long walk away. The nearest place may be a water-hole, stream or river some distance from the village. As they grow older, children are expected to balance ever bigger pots or tins on their heads. Women carry pots containing 15–20 litres of water, about the maximum weight a traveller is allowed to take on an aeroplane! Just to supply the family's basic needs, three or four journeys to the river may need to be made every day.

Carrying heavy loads of water regularly can have dangerous physical effects on young girls, such as changing the shape of the pelvis. This can make pregnancy and childbirth dangerous for them. The effort of water-carrying can use up their physical resources too – long journeys with heavy loads, especially if they are uphill, can burn up to 90 per cent of the food women eat each day.

Government and **aid agencies** are gradually bringing fresh water to more villages. Most cities have piped water supplies, except in the poorer suburbs and **shanty-towns**. In urban areas where there are no standpipes, water is often delivered by lorry and poured into a communal tank.

△ Collecting water from a standpipe in England during a period of cold weather when supplies to houses were frozen.

Even in developed countries, in times of drought the water supply to private homes may be turned off and standpipes installed in the streets.

WATER ON TAP

The water that flows out of your tap has been on a complicated journey before it reaches you. It has probably come from a **reservoir**, dug in a valley to catch and store water from hill streams, melted snow or surface water. From there it goes through an elaborate purifying process at a water treatment works. First it passes through several strainers and screens, and then through **sedimentation tanks**. The remaining particles in the water thicken when certain chemicals are added and are then allowed to settle. The water is filtered through beds of sand and, finally, disinfected with a chemical such as chlorine.

△ A reservoir in Zimbabwe. Reservoirs are natural or artificial lakes which are used for collecting and storing water.

One stage of a water treatment plant in the USA. Water passes through many purifying processes before it reaches our homes. ▽

The purified water is sometimes pumped into water storage towers, and from there it flows along pipes to our homes. Each house is connected to the **mains** by a service pipe on which there is a 'stopcock', or valve, which can be turned off if repairs need to be done.

Most developed countries now use and re-use their water supplies to gain as much benefit from them as possible. Water from lakes, rivers, reservoirs and wells is treated to make it drinkable, and dirty water is discharged to the sewers.

▽ How water is piped into, around and out of a house. The blue pipes carry cold water from the mains to the house, the red pipes carry hot water around the house, and the green pipes carry away the waste water.

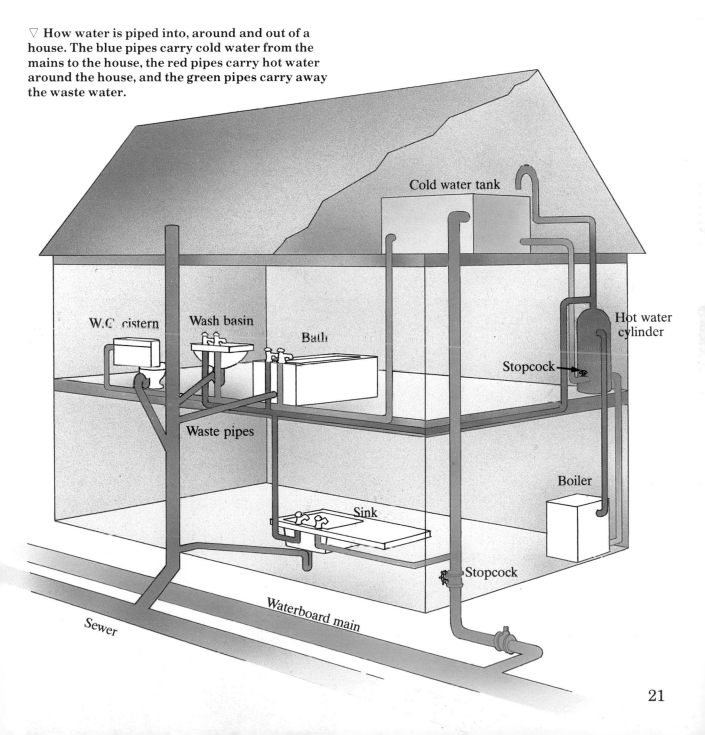

Cold water tank

W.C cistern

Wash basin

Bath

Hot water cylinder

Stopcock

Waste pipes

Boiler

Sink

Stopcock

Sewer

Waterboard main

21

CLEAN WATER, DIRTY WATER

Water can be purifying and life-giving. It can also be a carrier of disease and a cause of death. As it is such a good **solvent**, it can absorb both nourishing and harmful substances. In developed countries, dirty water from our homes and factories has to be carefully treated at a sewage works before it can be released into the rivers or the sea, to avoid pollution.

The World Health Organization has estimated that 80 per cent of the disease in the world today is caused by impure water and poor **sanitation**. Water-borne diseases kill over 30,000 children a day. One in six people in the world are affected and 5 million babies die every year.

There are several different kinds of water-borne disease. Some are caused by drinking infected water, others are passed on by touching infected people. Insects that breed in water can infect humans with disease. The biggest killers are diarrhoea, bilharzia and malaria. Bilharzia comes from infected snails which thrive in weedy streams and lakes. Their eggs eventually hatch into worms that bore into the skin of anyone who plays or works in the water. Bilharzia causes great misery and weakness.

▽ Women and children in Bangladesh wash their cooking pots in this river, which is also used for washing and watering animals, for bathing and for swimming.

Malaria is common in many of the hot, tropical parts of the world and is carried by mosquitoes, which breed in stagnant water. Diseases such as polio, cholera, typhoid and amoebic dysentry are all caused by bad sanitation.

Water and sanitation schemes can reduce the number of child deaths and the spread of diseases if, at the same time, people are educated about health. Aid organizations are concerned with ways of preventing disease, and with helping to cure people who are suffering now. A simple cure for diarrhoea, one of the major causes of death in under-five-year-olds, is to give them a solution consisting of water, sugar and salt. Of course the water used in this solution must be pure. In one village in Honduras, diarrhoea cases were reduced by 50 per cent after a campaign was started to encourage people to drink boiled water.

△ A clean, safe water supply has been piped to the children attending this school in Peru.

Water and sanitation schemes are being introduced in developing counries – this girl in Honduras is being washed from a hose attched to a new water supply. ▷

THE WATER DECADE

Without access to clean safe water, most of the world's children are prone to ill-health and millions fall victim to fatal diseases. The **United Nations** decided to launch a special campaign in the 1980s, called the International Drinking Water and Sanitation Decade. The aim was to provide clean water and sanitation for all by 1990. By 1985, 270 million people were able to obtain safe water for the first time. But if the original target was going to be reached, half a million people would have to be provided with new services every day throughout the period, and this was not possible.

Bringing clean water to a rural community may mean constructing a well, protecting existing wells or piping water from a stream. If a project is to succeed it must involve the villagers at every stage – from choosing the right site, to training them to use and maintain the equipment.

Aid agencies can work most effectively through village committees which organize the help of the villagers. In the Santa Barbara district of Honduras, Save the Children's specially trained water promoters visited villages to discuss a scheme to supply piped water. Villagers provided all the labour and were supplied with the equipment they were unable to afford. The scheme has helped education as well as health. As one schoolgirl said, 'We can stay on at school now that we don't have to walk miles to the river each day to fetch water.'

In the village of Palugaswewa in Sri Lanka a community well was desperately needed but villagers could not afford to take time off from the 'chena', which is the cutting and burning of the forest to provide land for cultivation. The problem was solved by paying the villagers enough to live on while they built the well. The money was provided by WaterAid, a charity created by the organizations within the British water industry.

Three out of every four people in the developing world have no kind of proper sanitation. Even when **latrines** are installed, disease may not be reduced unless people are taught rules of hygiene. An important contribution to health education is made by the Child-to-Child programme which involves older children teaching hygienic habits to younger ones.

◁ **Women working at a footpump well near their village in Burkina Faso, West Africa.**

24

A Honduran woman enjoying the luxury of water piped to her home. △

◁ Many people in developing countries have no proper sanitation – these latrines have been built near an Ethiopian village and will help reduce disease.

FIGHTING POLLUTION

There are many serious dangers created by pollution, which are a threat to children and adults all over the world. The Earth itself is being poisoned. The water in many rivers, lakes and oceans, and even in rainfall, is being **contaminated**. There are many causes of water pollution. Rivers can be polluted by animal waste and artificial fertilizers that are washed off the land, and by industrial waste containing harmful chemicals. All these combine to kill the fish that live in the rivers, which means that a valuable source of food is destroyed and many people lose their livelihood.

The sea is being polluted, too. Oil-tankers sometimes leak and spill their contents into the water or illegally clean out their tanks at sea. As a result, great slicks of oil are washed ashore, spoiling beaches. Sea birds die if oil clogs their feathers or if they eat fish contaminated by oil. Raw or only partly-treated sewage is discharged into the sea in many places, too. In recent years, **radioactive** waste from nuclear power stations and the nuclear weapons industry has been dumped at sea.

Another threat to our planet is acid rain. Acids from factories, power stations and car exhausts are expelled into the atmosphere and this contaminates the rainfall. Acid rain falls on rivers, lakes, forests, buildings and crops. Thousands of lakes and rivers in Scandinavia are dying, and half the forests of West Germany have been destroyed.

Organizations like Greenpeace and Friends of the Earth campaign against destruction of the environment. Governments are gradually taking steps to reduce pollution but often the interests of industry and business do not coincide with the demands of ordinary people, who want to preserve their planet for the following generations.

△ **When oil is discharged from tankers, the thick sludgy mass is washed ashore where it destroys plant and animal life.**

△ Industrial pollution in the River Athi, downstream from Nairobi in Kenya.

Gases from industry and cars combine in the atmosphere to fall as acid rain which damages trees, lakes and buildings. ▽

FISHING COMMUNITIES

If you look at a map of the Pacific Ocean you will see many clusters of islands – the Solomon Islands, the Caroline Islands, the New Hebrides, the Phoenix Islands and the Hawaiian Islands, to name only a few. Some of these **archipelagoes** consist of thousands of islands. Some are uninhabited but others are populated by communities who depend on the sea for their welfare and survival. The life of coastal communities on the continental mainlands also depends on the sea.

▽ **A fisherman on an Indonesian island inspects his nets before setting out to sea.**

In many island and coastal communities tourism has become an important industry. However, many people still depend on fishing for their livelihood. So it is vitally important to keep the seas of the world free from pollution.

Fishing was the earliest form of hunting and fish was the first flesh food eaten by human beings. Some fish are immensely important, not just as a source of protein, but for other reasons too. For example, nutritious oils are obtained from the liver of the halibut, the cod and the shark.

Fishing is also important for people living near inland waterways and lakes. In the freezing wastes of the polar regions children learn to fish through holes in the ice, and catch the food that keeps them alive.

Fishing has become big business, controlled – especially in the deep seas – by the fleets of the world's richest and most powerful nations. The United Nations' Law of the Sea gives countries the exclusive right to their coastal waters, up to an agreed distance, for fishing and for extracting oil and minerals from the sea-bed. But many developing countries lack the money to exploit their offshore waters fully.

Gutting and filleting fish for market on the Caribbean island of Barbados. △

◁ Off the coast of Victoria in Australia, a fisherman loads his boat with traps to catch crayfish.

WATER FOR AGRICULTURE

Most of the world's children live in the countryside, where people depend directly on the land for their survival. Children often help with the crops and look after the animals. If they do not go to school this can be a full-time job.

Most plants need large quantities of water for each stage of their growth. Growing enough wheat to bake a loaf of bread, for example, takes 435 litres of water. Some crops need much more water than others. Rice is grown in water-logged paddy fields, and cotton, which needs twice as much water as rice, can only be grown in tropical lands with a very high rainfall.

◁ **Mechanical overhead water sprayers are used to irrigate crops in France.**

Working in a paddy field in the Philippines. Rice needs a great deal of water and can only be grown in areas with a high rainfall. ▽

Problems are often caused by shortage of water. If there is not enough rain, farmers have to **irrigate** their fields. Irrigation systems normally involve diverting water from a reservoir or river and directing it into a network of ditches and channels that run through the agricultural land. In developed countries overhead spraying of crops is another common irrigation method. The USA uses 416 billion litres of water each day for irrigation – that is enough to fill a lake 8 kilometres long, 1.5 kilometres wide and 300 metres deep.

Irrigation does not always benefit the poorest people in developing countries. If a dam is built and a large area of land flooded by the dam's reservoir, people are forced to leave their homes – the four biggest dams built in Africa have claimed one-and-a-half million homes since they were built. The irrigated land is often used for growing cash crops for export rather than food for local people.

The cost of maintaining big irrigation projects can be met by charging farmers for the water. To pay these charges farmers have to grow crops to sell rather than to eat themselves. As a result these farmers may get into debt through buying seeds and fertilizers, and into still further debt if the price of the crop falls. Meanwhile they will have neglected their own food crops. Irrigation channels can also increase the risk of malaria, bilharzia and other water-borne diseases.

When the rains fail, drought occurs. During the African drought of 1984–5 millions of people died of famine. But drought need not always cause famine. Africa could feed itself even in times of

△ Women in Honduras painstakingly water their crops by hand.

drought if food production had not been so neglected for so long. Unfortunately, the poorest people have the least control over the way land and water is used.

WATER FOR INDUSTRY

Vast quantities of water are used in industry. 150,000 litres are used up in the production of just one tonne of steel. To make one tonne of newsprint 750,000 litres are needed. Industry is charged for water according to how much is used. To keep down costs, factories re-use water several times. Power stations use a great deal of water to cool down the huge output of heat which is produced.

Children in developed countries, and almost everywhere in the developing world, use goods every day that have been produced in factories using water for many important processes.

If you live in a highly industrialized country like the USA, you use an enormous number of manufactured goods every day. Think about a typical day. The clothes you put on in the morning have been mass-produced in factories. Much of the food you consume has been processed, and comes out of packets or tins which are also produced in factories. You may go to school by bus or car; you use books, videos and laboratory equipment in class, all of which are manufactured.

▽ **Power stations use vast amounts of water for their cooling systems.**

At the end of the school day it's time for recreation. Do you watch television? Go roller-skating? Play games? If you are thirsty after an energetic game, perhaps you have a soft drink, or eat a juicy apple! Unless you picked the apple from a tree, the chances are that even this has come to you via a factory. Water is used to wash the fruit and also to move it from one place to another like a kind of conveyor belt.

Water is added to many foodstuffs. It is the main ingredient in most soft drinks. Water and wood form the pulp from which paper for books, newspapers and cartons are made. Whatever the goods being manufactured – clothes, vehicles, televisions, video recorders, baseballs or roller-skates – a large amount of water is used to cool down the machinery used on the production line.

△ Many soft drinks are manufactured by a process using large amounts of water.

Manufacturing industry uses a huge amount of water. For instance, this paper-making machine is part of a process which uses as much water in a day as the population of a small town. ▽

WATER FOR POWER

Hundreds of years ago people realized that they could harness the force and energy of rushing water for their own use. The water wheel, which is thought to have been invented in China, was for centuries one of the two principal means of obtaining power (the other being the windmill). A water wheel is turned by the force of water flowing on to it. A horizontal shaft, which extends from the centre of the wheel, drives machinery.

▽ One of the earliest forms of power was the water wheel. This one has been used for centuries to turn millstones for grinding corn.

Nowadays we use water power to generate electricity. This is known as **hydroelectric power**. Water is stored in huge quantities behind a dam and builds up to an extremely high pressure. It is released down a tunnel on to a turbine – a modern and more efficient version of the water wheel – which turns a shaft leading to a generator to create electricity.

Power stations also rely on water. In coal-fired power stations coal is burned to heat water which turns into steam and drives the turbines.

Many developing countries have built hydroelectric power stations in recent years. Dams and hydroelectric power stations are extremely expensive to build and – as in the case of irrigation projects – may not help the poorest people. Developing countries are often faced with a choice between improving the lives of communities, such as the introduction of sanitation and clean water projects – and expensive large-scale industrial projects. Most aid agencies are concerned with small-scale projects to help people gain control over their own local environment.

Tidal power stations could be an important development in the future. Although they are expensive to build, they are cheap to run. Oil has become very costly, coal stocks will eventually run out, and nuclear power is not acceptable to everyone. Many people, therefore, are concerned about a safe, healthy environment, and are looking for alternative sources of energy.

△ A huge dam in British Columbia, Canada. Water is released from the reservoir on to the blades of a turbine which will power a generator to produce electricity.

△ The tidal power station at Rance in France. Electricity is produced by the power of the incoming and outgoing tides.

TRANSPORT BY WATER

Very few children have gone on such hazardous sea journeys as those who left the shores of Vietnam with their families in the 1970s, in search of a safe refuge in other parts of the world. These refugees, who fled their country for political reasons, came to be known as the Boat People. Hundreds of thousands of people set sail on the China Sea, and out of desperation used small boats which were unsuitable for the rough weather of the high seas. Most were picked up by large ocean-going ships and taken to Hong Kong, Europe or North America.

Ever since humankind learnt to build boats from hollowed-out tree trunks, the seas and the waterways have been used for transport, trade and communication. The world was first 'opened up' through sea travel. Explorers and traders established contacts between distant countries and continents. Flourishing trading ports grew up along the coasts and **navigable** parts of inland waterways.

In many developing countries today where there are few roads, rivers are busy highways, carrying people and goods to places that cannot easily be reached in any other way. The West African country of Gambia is named after the river that flows through it. There are few tarred roads in the country and until recently, the river was essential for the transport of medical supplies and other goods.

Canals have been vital in opening up wider communications. Some, like the Panama Canal and the Suez Canal, have greatly shortened the length of sea journeys. In many developed countries there is an extensive network of canals and rivers, allowing a cheap and efficient means of transport. The Rhine–Main–Danube waterway is one of the busiest in Europe, and the St. Lawrence Seaway is a very busy waterway in Canada.

▽ **This river in Bangladesh proves the best method of transport for a health worker.**

Today, communications between all parts of the globe have been transformed by air travel and many forms of new technology. But heavy or bulky goods are still sent between continents by sea. Huge oil tankers, for example, have become a familiar sight on the oceans.

△ **(inset) Oil tankers, and other huge freight carriers transport cargoes across the oceans.**

△ The large picture above shows a lock on the busy Welland Canal – part of the St Lawrence Seaway in Canada, which allows shipping to reach deep into North America.

WATER AND BELIEF

Water plays an important part in all the world's religions. In ancient mythology water is often believed to be the source of life. In many religions, baptism, a ritual purifying in water, is the first religious ceremony that a child experiences.

Many rivers and springs have been thought to be sacred. **Immersion** in such rivers as the Euphrates (Iraq), the Jordan (Israel and Syria), the Tiber (Italy), the Nile (Egypt) or the Ganges (India) – was believed to cure a person of disease and to purify them from sin. In the Christian religion, the town of Lourdes in southern France is a special place of pilgrimage, especially for the sick. There, the Virgin Mary is believed to have appeared to a young girl called Bernadette and shown her a miraculous stream which would heal the sick.

▽ **Many Hindus believe that the water of the River Ganges is sacred, and they come from all over India to bathe in it.**

△ **A priest of the Balinese-Hindu religion, in Indonesia, cleanses people with holy water.**

In many places, towns (called spas) have grown up where mineral springs or hot sulphur wells have been discovered. In ancient Eygpt many of the temples dedicated to the god of medicine were built next to mineral springs.

Water is also associated with a much more dramatic and violent form of cleansing. Stories of a Great Flood are widespread. The Flood was believed to have been a punishment for sin, a way of destroying a disobedient people and cleansing the world. In Jewish and Christian legends only Noah and his family, and two of every species of animal and bird, survived the fateful deluge.

Water is also seen as a force that brings life. Water moistens the earth and makes plants grow and bear fruit. It revives vegetation after drought. In Cameroon, West Africa, the corn festival of the Bamessing people is celebrated in the dry season. It begins with the mourning of the dead vegetation. The god who gave nourishment has died. The people believe that the chief symbolically 'dies' with the god and has to be brought back to life with miraculous 'chieftain water'.

△ Cleansing by water is an important Muslim ritual. This Muslim is washing his feet before entering the mosque.

A baby being baptized in the Christening ceremony of the Christian Church. ▽

WATER FOR PLEASURE

△ **Wind-surfing off a beach near Sydney in Australia.**

Not only is water essential for all life, it also gives us pleasure and enjoyment in many different ways. Most people enjoy the sensation of water on their bodies, whether they are relaxing in a bath or standing under a shower, swimming in the sea or in a heated pool. In some developed countries, particularly the USA, **jacuzzi** baths have become tremendously popular in recent years.

Think of the number of water sports there are. In addition to swimming, there is canoeing, rowing, sailing, speed-boating, water-skiing, surfboarding, wind-surfing and water polo. Angling is also a very popular sport.

Winter sports, such as skiing, tobogganning, bobsleigh-riding, ice-skating and ice-hockey, all depend on the freezing of water.

Water also offers some of the most beautiful and impressive natural sights for people to enjoy. Peaceful lakes, quiet streams, wide rivers, dramatic waterfalls and the sea in its many changing moods, can all be sources of wonder and fascination. Water – particularly the play of light on water – is a favourite subject for many artists and photographers.

Few children in the developing world can share the same enjoyment of water as children in developed countries, because it is too much a part of their survival.

40

The natural beauty of a peaceful lakeland scene attracts many people away from their busy city lives, in search of tranquility. ▽

▽ Children play happily in a pool in Swaziland.

THE FUTURE

The demand for water is growing all the time. By the 1980s it was twice as high as it was in the 1960s. In July 1987 the world population reached 5 billion. It is expected that the population for the year 2000 will be over 6 billion, and for the year 2025 it will be over 8 billion. By then the goals of the 1980s Water Decade will be totally out of date. But the alarming rate of population increase is part of a vicious circle in developing countries, of poverty, disease and a high death rate amongst babies and young children. Unless conditions improve for poor people; unless they gain control over the resources they need; unless the need for clean safe water – amongst many other things – is met, families will go on having large families as a kind of insurance against their children dying.

△ Water can be educational as well as fun. These children are learning wet and dry sensations and about pouring.

▽ The Bhakra Nangal Dam on the River Ganges in India provides water for irrigation and power, and controls the water supply at times of flood and low rainfall.

The demand for water is also constantly increased by the growth of industry in many parts of the world. Many countries in South America and South-east Asia are fast becoming industrialized. As we have seen, the demands of industry may well conflict with the needs of ordinary people. The important question for the future is 'What kind of development?' This includes vital questions about control of water supplies as well as other resources.

We talk about 'developed' and 'developing' countries but these words are not very accurate. There are many people in so-called developed countries living without bathrooms or a reliable clean water supply, and in poor conditions generally. The industrialized, developed world has to learn to conserve water instead of wasting it. It has to stop poisoning the rivers, the sea and the atmosphere – otherwise there will be no future for any of us.

Water is one of the world's most precious resources. The challenge to find more water, to distribute it fairly and to keep it clean is greater than ever before.

△ The pump where these Indian women and children are collecting water is the most important place in their village.

GLOSSARY

Aid agency An organization that works to improve the health and living conditions of people in need.

Archipelago A group of islands.

Artesian basin A layer of porous rock between two impermeable layers, which becomes saturated with water.

Contaminated Polluted, made dirty and spoilt by sewage, chemicals or other waste.

Developed and developing countries The poorer, underdeveloped countries including most of Africa, Asia and Central and South America, and the contrasting rich, industrialized nations of Western Europe, North America, Japan and Australasia.

Foetus The developing baby inside the womb.

Immersion Being dipped under the surface of the water.

Hydroelectric power The generation of electricity by the pressure of falling water.

Impermeable Not allowing water to pass through or be absorbed.

Irrigate To bring water to dry land.

Jacuzzi A small bath or tub with underwater jets which massage the body and improve circulation.

Lachrymal gland A gland at the outer corner of the eye that causes tears to flow.

Latrine A lavatory.

Navigable A waterway that is wide, deep and safe enough to take shipping.

Nutrient A nourishing substance.

Porous Allowing water to soak in or pass through (opposite of impermeable).

Protein Substances which are present in foods such as milk, eggs, meat, fish and cheese, and which are an essential part of our diet.

Radioactive Giving off energy in the form of electromagnetic rays, which can be highly dangerous.

Reservoir An artificial lake used for storing water.

Sanitation The use of proper arrangements for drainage, rubbish disposal, cleanliness etc, to protect health.

Sedimentation tanks Special tanks that allow sewage to sink to the bottom and be removed.

Shanty-town A poor area, with bad housing and poor living conditions on the outskirts of a city.

Solvent A substance capable of dissolving another substance.

United Nations International organization of independent states founded in 1945 to promote peace and international co-operation.

Water mains The main distribution network for water.

Water table The surface of the water-saturated part of the ground. It usually follows the contours of the overlying land surface.

As a substance, and as a topic for children to explore, water is extremely versatile. Since water is everywhere, in different forms and performing different functions, children will be able to think of plenty of ways in which it is used by themselves and other people. This provides a good starting point from which to move on to aspects of the topic which may be less familiar to them – the use of water in industry, for example, or the severe problems of water-related diseases in the developing world.

There is plenty of scope for activity. Children could try going through a whole day using only 12 litres of water, the average amount used daily by people in developing countries. With the help of a science teacher perhaps, they could carry out simple experiments such as demonstrating evaporation, water pressure, how water can be filtered through sand, or how a simple waterwheel works. It may be possible to organize outings to farms, factories, water treatment works or even sewage works, so that children can see for themselves how water is used and treated in these places.

Water is an excellent subject for cross-curriculum work. Science has already been mentioned. The centrality of the topic to geography is equally obvious. A historical approach will also enhance children's appreciation of the way water crucially affects the quality of life. For instance, cholera, typhoid and other water-borne diseases were commonplace in Europe and North America until only about 100 years ago. History can also show how water can affect relations between nations – the Suez crisis in 1956 brought the world to the brink of war.

The book touches on the importance of water in religion and legend, and this could obviously be explored further. There is a wealth of poetry, stories and songs about rain, rivers, lakes, the sea, drinking and thirst, floods and drought. These would give a further imaginative dimension to the subject and could help stimulate creative writing and art work.

In the last chapter it is pointed out that the terms 'developed' and 'developing' are inadequate to describe different parts of the world. It is most important that children do not equate less developed countries with misery, poverty, disease and nothing else. They should be encouraged to look for the positive and impressive aspects of people's lives in the developing world. Many of these can be inferred from the text: for instance; the patience and endurance of women and children who have to walk miles each day in search of water; the hard work and sense of community that enable a village to provide all the labour for bringing piped water from a distant stream; the courage of children and adults in the face of debilitating disease.

The addresses and resources listed on the following pages are just a selection. If children do write for further information, they are advised to enclose a large, stamped, self-addressed envelope.

USEFUL ADDRESSES

In Britain

Appropriate Health Resources and Technologies Action Group
85 Marylebone High Street, London W1.

CAFOD
2 Garden Close, London SW9 9TY.

Centre for World Development Education (CWDE)
Regent's College, Regent's Park, London NW1.

Christian Aid
P.O. Box 9, London SW9 8BH.

Commonwealth Institute
Kensington High Street, London W8 6NQ.

Friends of the Earth
377 City Road, London EC1V 1NA.

Intermediate Technology Development Group
9 King Street, London WC2.

International Broadcasting Trust
2 Ferdinand Place, London NW1.
Supplies videos (with teachers' notes and other print material) on world development issues.

National Association of Development Education Centres (NADEC)
6 Endsleigh Street, London WC1H 0DX.
Will supply an address list of development education centres in Britain.

Oxfam
274 Banbury Road, Oxford OX2 7DZ.

Overseas Development Administration
Eland House, Stag Place, London SW1.

Panos
8 Alfred Place, London WC1.
Stocks resources on environmental concerns.

Save the Children
Mary Datchelor House, 17 Grove Lane, London SE5 8RD.

UK Committee for UNICEF
55 Lincoln's Inn Fields, London WC2.

War on Want
37–39 Great Guildford Street, London SE1 0ES.

WaterAid
1 Queen Anne's Gate, London SW1H 9BT.

World Development Movement
Bedford Chambers, Covent Garden, London WC2E 8HA.

In Australia

Australian Development Assistance Bureau
GPO Box 887, Canberra ACT 2601

In Canada

Canadian International Development Agency
Ottawa, K 1A0G4

BOOKS TO READ

For younger readers

Focus on water by Mark Corliss (Wayland, 1985).

Let's Imagine: Water by Tom Johnston (The Bodley Head, 1985).

Looking at Water by J. Sowry (Batsford, 1982).

The Book of Water by P. Carpi (ed) (Benn, 1980).

Water by T. Jennings (Oxford University Press, 1982).

The Water from Your Tap by Julian Fox (Wayland, 1982).

World Health by Janie Hampton (Wayland, 1987).

Resources

New Internationalist No. 103, September 1981. Whole issue devoted to subject of water.

Water, Sanitation, Health – for all? Prospects for the *International Drinking Water Supply and Sanitation Decade* by Anil Agarwal *et al.* (Earthscan, 1982)

The following materials are just a selection available from WaterAid (see Useful Addresses). Write for a full catalogue.

Posters:
Please help her (showing effects of insufficient water).
Please help him (showing ill-effects of playing in dirty water).
Water – the problems.
Water – some of the solutions (featuring hand pumps and ventilated latrines).

Audiovisuals available on loan:
For want of water film (Shell Film Unit, 25 mins, colour).
Journey for survival film (UN, 15 mins, colour) on the Water Decade and featuring material from Ethiopia, Yemen, Peru, India, Bangladesh and the Philippines.
WaterAid in East Africa slide-tape set.
Water and sanitation: basic needs, slide-tape set, introduction to some of the problems of the Water Decade and some of the solutions.
Working in Sierra Leone video cassette (Northumbrian Water/Tyne-Tees Television, 25 mins).

There are also a number of other slide sets available from WaterAid.

PICTURE CREDITS

INDEX

Page numbers that refer to illustrations are in **bold**.